Contents

1. WHY I WROTE THIS
2. HOW DEBT COMES ABOUT
3. GROUNDHOG DAY
4. HABITS AND CYCLES
5. THE DEBT SPIRAL
6. ONE STEP AT A TIME
7. STARING DOWN THE PROBLEM
8. ALL CARDS ON THE TABLE
9. FACING THE FEAR
10. TIME FOR A PLAN
11. Know what you owe
12. THERE IS ALWAYS TIME
13. TALKING IT OVER
14. REELING IT IN
15. COMING OUT STRONGER

1. WHY I WROTE THIS

I have been in debt since I was 19 years old. I am now 49. And, now, debt-free. That's 30 years of owing money to others. To banks, loan companies, credit card companies, landlords, family members and friends.
Over a quarter of a century of watching the largest part of my pay packet drain away before my very eyes.
Years of watching every penny. Fretting over the cost of everything. Worrying over every bit of expenditure.
And by 'debt', I don't mean that the bank took a regular cut of my pay each month to pay off a home mortgage.
I don't mean that I had a credit card or store card that I failed to pay off in full every month.
I didn't have a mortgage. I rented. And I still do.
I didn't even have a store card.
But I did have many credit cards. And a hefty serial bank loan.
I've learnt every trick to escape the landlord's footsteps.
Hiding the bank's demand letters.
Avoiding the credit card company's aggressive phone calls.
Lying to my creditors? A monthly occurrence.
Paying one bill while begging an extension on another? Easy.
Withdrawing cash on my credit cards mid-month? I treated them like debit cards.
I've had as many as five credit cards, bumping against the limits every month, as I paid almost nothing back. I had no idea what they were costing me - I needed that credit, that dribble of cash. Often to pay off some other credit.
I know full well that constant knot in the stomach. The continuous tension, the worry and – yes – the icy, hard fear. I use the word 'fear'.
Those who live debt-free may not know that the phrase 'waking up in a cold sweat' is actually true. The mind flooded with panic as you try to think of a way to

get through the following day, the week, the month. Who do I have to lie to today? Whose phone call do I ignore? Where do I have to hide when the doorbell rings? Have you scraped up loose change from under every bit of furniture, from every pocket? Have you written a check to 'cash' in the first week of the month? Do you know every payday loan outlet within walking distance of your home? Then you know the tight, gnawing, ever-present, draining effect of debt.

In case you're wondering, since leaving College, back in the late 1980s, I've never been out of a job. Fired? Made redundant or 'let go'? Several times. But I've never had more than a few weeks where I've had to wonder where the next salary is coming from.

I've earned a good salary for the past twenty years. An amount that should support a family and a mortgage in a decent-sized home in comfort. I've earned enough that I shouldn't have had to use my company Amex to pay for groceries towards the end of the month.

I don't gamble, I don't drink to excess, I don't have a drug habit – I don't even have a shopping habit, for goodness sake! So why am I always head-over-heels in debt?

In this short book, I look into why we get into debt, why it's so difficult to get out of debt and how you can finally be free of it for the rest of your life.

I'll give you the benefit of my experience. I hope that I can help you find the peace of mind that I now have.

2. HOW DEBT COMES ABOUT

There are many reasons why people fall into debt.
It's important to realize that debtors come from all walks of life. All income brackets, all social backgrounds, faiths and cultures fall into debt.
The deep heartache, stress, fear and sheer pain of debt is all the fault of the debtor. That's what people who have never experienced debt say. They say that people should have looked after their cash better. That they shouldn't have spent more than they earn. That they shouldn't have over-borrowed. That they shouldn't have relied on easy credit that they couldn't pay back. whether through loans or credit cards.
"Neither a borrower or a lender be."

This is old Polonius's advice to his son Laertes in Shakespeare's tragic play, 'Hamlet'. Sound advice, when viewed in a rear-view mirror.
Not much use if you are already drowning in a deep sea of debt.
Only someone who has been in the depths of despair that debt brings with it can understand how it feels. And what took them down that path.
It could have been wider family problems. Sickness in the family. A divorce. God forbid, the death of a loved one. It could have been the loss of a job at a crucial time – or at any time.
It could also be, let's face it, a simple problem of not being able to face the reality of the situation one is in.
None of us starts our lives in debt. None of us grows up and spends our childhoods and teenage years in debt. Our parents might have been in debt. Did we grow up in poverty? Or did we grow up in middle-class comfort, educated at the best schools? None of this is a guarantee against falling into debt later in life.
But whatever the circumstances that led you into debt, only one person can help you get out of it. Only one person can affect what happens next. With one person's

actions, you can start the steady rise from the dark depths of debt despair.

That one person, as you might have guessed, is the person closest to you. The person who knows you best. The person who has been with you throughout your whole life, come rain and shine, triumph and despair. The person who was with you every step as the debt mounted. You can guess who I'm referring to.

That person is you.

Now, I know that you may have a loving partner, close family or loyal friends. You might have a caring counsellor or pastor. Someone who can be a shoulder to lean on in troubled times.

They can help you, support you, encourage you and cheer you on from the sidelines.

But they are not you.

Many of you will not have any support network at all.

And that's OK.

After all, this fight – and it will be a fight – is going to be down to you.

I also understand you might feel that the debt was not brought on by your actions. Circumstances in your life might have caused the debt to come about. Events over which you had no control. Expenditure by you or by others which was necessary at the time.

Well, that's OK too.

Now, though. You must take charge.

The cavalry is coming to the rescue over the horizon.

And the cavalry is you.

If that comes as a shock, don't worry. I'll support you with tips and advice and personal insights from my own journey.

I'll be your wingman on this one.

3. GROUNDHOG DAY

Do you remember the classic Bill Murray movie, 'Groundhog Day'?

Bill plays a cynical TV weatherman. He goes to the small town of Punxsutawney to film a report about their annual Groundhog Day. And finds himself reliving the same day over and over again.

Bill's character gets more and more desperate.

"What would you do if you were stuck in one place, and every day was the same, and nothing you did mattered?" he exclaims at one point.

This is how life feels when you're in debt. Like you're stuck in an endless, loop. Doomed to repeat the same terrible days. The same situations – and the same mistakes – forever.

We can't deny that breaking the debt spiral will be hard to do. Very hard.

I'm going to go out on a limb here and say it will be one of the hardest things you've ever done in your life.

You might say that I'm being too simplistic. Is getting out of debt more difficult than graduating from college? Giving birth? Raising a child? Finding a job? You might think that giving up smoking was the toughest thing you ever did. Or even kicking a drug habit. You might even be a recovering alcoholic.

Let me say straight away that every one of those life events is important. All are hard. But let's also admit that getting out of debt is right up there with those.

Why? Because being in constant debt affects your life every day. It affects your physical health. It affects your mental state. It breaks up families and friends. It causes homelessness. It can lead to two of the states we mentioned above – alcohol and drug abuse. Financial troubles (let's read debt) are the major cause of divorce in the US and in many other countries.

4. HABITS AND CYCLES

We have established that getting out of debt is a priority, but we need to know that debt is a habit.

Not all habits are bad habits. But bad habits, once established, are far more difficult to crack than good habits are to put in place.

Think of some of your bad habits. Simple ones. Coming home from work, cracking a beer, switching on the TV and spending the evening on the sofa. Or pressing the 'snooze' button on your alarm clock – once, twice, three times. Or taking the elevator when your workplace or apartment is on the second floor. Simple right?

Now imagine changing those habits.

Come home from work, change into your sneakers, go back out and go for a walk or a run.

Set your alarm clock five minutes earlier and get out of bed at the first call.

Take the stairs up to your workplace or apartment instead of the elevator.

Now you've imagined it do it. Go, on, get up and go right out of the door and walk.

Not so easy, huh?

Well, debt is a habit like that. You might say, well that's not so tough. I can handle that. I could do any one or all those of those things. But actually, doing it is tougher than you think.

Do you smoke? Well, that's OK – that's another topic for another time! But I mention it here because I used to work with a couple of guys who were heavy smokers.

When I first started working with them, one of the guys said to me "It's OK though, son. I'm giving up right after the weekend. In fact, this will be my last packet." "That's great!" I replied "Good for you."

About a week later, I caught up with him in the yard. He was puffing away. "I thought you were going to quit!" I said. "Oh, I am" he replied. "In fact, this is my last packet."

I smiled to myself and walked away.

That's all well and good, you say, but what does it have to do with debt?

I tell that story, not because I'm a rabid anti-smoker. You can smoke all you want, as long as you keep me out of it! It's an illustration – an example, if you like.

At its simplest, let's say that 'old habits die hardest'. We are all creatures of habit, good and bad, after all.

Our habit might be smoking, like my two colleagues, or it might be working too hard at the office.

It might be a quiet beer on the way home from work, standing at the same end of the same bar.

It might be picking up a good book for an hour before bed.

So, let's be clear what we mean. Debt is a habit. And it's not a good habit.

5. THE DEBT SPIRAL

We slide into debt without noticing. It starts small. Like that first smoke behind the bathroom block at school.
A few dollars borrowed from a friend and not repaid. A small bank overdraft here, a loan from the bank there, a few car repairs on the credit card.
But it builds and builds. One tiny step at a time.
Pretty soon, a habit is forming. The overdraft grows. We forget that it's also a debt. One day we get the monthly pay check and it doesn't cover the overdraft.
(We forget that an overdraft is a debt, like an *expensive* personal loan.)
Then the bank offers us a 'consolidation' loan to take care of the overdraft and the credit card.
But we don't cut up the card.
And soon we're back in the spiral again. Except this time we have the consolidation loan, an overdraft and the credit cards.
The spiral has begun again.
Once the habit imprints on the brain, it's difficult to get rid of.
Wait, you ask "You said you worked with a couple of smokers – what happened to the other guy? Well. He used to smoke at least 80 cigarettes a day.
The ashtray on his desk (back then, you could smoke in offices) was always full to overflowing. He used to replace it several times a day.

Then one day, he quit. Like that. He hasn't smoked in almost 20 years. Sure, he went through a bad patch when he took to eating candy instead and ballooned in weight. But now he's slim and well – and looks 20 years younger.
And the first guy, well he finally quit too. A couple of years ago. After his surgeon told him that if he didn't, the recurring bronchitis he kept on getting would soon kill him.
Quitting a habit immediately, like the other smoker, is difficult. And that won't

work for everyone. In fact, unless you have that kind of personality, don't go for that option!

Have you or someone you love ever had trouble with their weight? Then you know that the 'instant weight loss' plan rarely works. Drinking diet shakes. Cutting down your calorie intake to almost nil. These are not long-term solutions. Unless your career relies on maintaining a specific weight. Like a professional boxer or jockey.

As we will see later on, it will take a little time to untangle ourselves from the debt habit. But a little time taken now will ensure a more lasting reward.

At the end of the movie, Bill Murray's character in 'Groundhog Day' manages to turn the situation to his advantage.

In my story about the smokers, the first guy's surgeon was his wake-up call.

Who's your 'surgeon' when it comes to debt? If you're reading this, then I would suggest that you know who your surgeon is.

It's you.

6. ONE STEP AT A TIME

Al Pacino spoke to his team as inspirational football coach Tony D'Amato in the movie 'Any Given Sunday':

"We're in hell right now gentlemen. Believe me. And we can stay here, get the s*** kicked out of us, or we can fight our way back into the light. We can climb outta hell... one inch at a time."

Kicking a habit, and establishing a new one at the same one, is difficult. But getting on the path to changing a habit is easy.

And this applies to many things in life.

It only takes you doing one thing. One single thing.

You could do it today. You could do it right now. This minute. This second.

Or you could settle deeper into that armchair. Fire up Facebook. Say to yourself that you'll start tomorrow.

So, what is that simple thing? Well, it's so simple that it will shock you. You'll kick yourself. It's something that everyone can do, whatever their condition.

That simple thing is:

Do something.

Move forward.

Take one action.

The Chinese philosopher Lao Tzu said

"A journey of a thousand miles starts with a single step."

He said that around 2600 years ago. And it still applies to many, many aspects of our lives. But it especially applies to the challenge you have facing you now.

"One small step for a man, one giant leap for mankind."

So proclaimed Neil Armstrong as he put the first human foot onto the surface of the moon.

We can say the same for you on your personal journey. You're going to take a small step forward.

And it's going to change your life forever.

It won't make much of a difference to *mankind*, but it will to you.
Because another step will follow.
And another, and another, and another.
And then you'll be unstoppable!

And you'll achieve your goal of a debt-free life.
That's certainly one giant leap to look forward to.

7. STARING DOWN THE PROBLEM

The father of a good friend of mine was on his way back home from a trip.
He was in his early 60s and generally in good health.
He arrived at his hometown railway station. It was a pleasant Spring day and he decided to walk the 3 miles or so to his house.

As he set out across town, he began to feel a little unwell. At first a little nauseous, he took no heed, thinking it was something he ate on the train.
He walked on.
He began to feel a little indigestion coming on.
Again, he walked on – must have been that pickle sandwich at lunch for sure.

Further on he felt a sharp pain in his left arm followed by a tingle in the fingers of his left hand. Well, this isn't great, he thought, but it's only a couple of miles home and then I'll take a nap for a while.
By the time he opened his front door, an hour or so later, he was perspiring and couldn't catch his breath.
His wife, shocked by his appearance – now grey-faced, asked what was up. As he explained his symptoms, she sat him down in the living room and grabbed the phone to call 911.
"I need help!" she cried "My husband is having a heart attack!"
A paramedic team was there within 15 minutes. By this time, the situation was critical. Luckily, they were able to stabilize him and transferred him to the nearest hospital.
Things calmed down. He settled in a hospital bed.
His wife asked him "Why did you walk all the way home? Why didn't you call 911 or ask someone to do it for you?"
His response "Oh, I didn't want to bother anyone. I didn't think it was anything to

worry about."

Luckily, following surgery, my friend's father made a good recovery. But he had had a very lucky escape.

And his doctor has told him many times now, at the onset of any symptoms – you get yourself to a hospital, immediately.

Well, that was a rather long way to illustrate a very important point.

Ignoring a problem won't make it go away.

In fact, the longer you pretend it isn't happening, the worse it will get. This applies in all walks of life, of course, and in many situations.

I can't imagine any situation in which ignoring a problem is likely to make it better, turn it around or solve it.

You may say that my friend's dad didn't know there was a problem. The hell he didn't.

He had a good idea that those symptoms weren't leading to a great situation. But he was so scared of what might be about to happen, that he tried to walk on as if nothing was happening.

Hoping to get home, close his eyes and have it all cleared up overnight.

He was fortunate.

He didn't end up a victim of a severe and life-changing stroke. He could even have died. Because he was unwilling to face down what is a common problem. One that would have posed little drama for the emergency operator or the paramedics.

As his doctor says, *"In these cases, every minute counts."*

And, of course, the same applies to debt. The longer we pretend that we're not in debt. The longer we ignore it. The worse it gets.

Interest rates for debt, especially unauthorized debt, are always punitive, if not positively criminal.

When we decide to face up to the problem, we can move forward at last and set ourselves to the challenge of clearing it up.

Once we do that, I can tell you from personal experience, the world begins to look a very much brighter place indeed.

8. ALL CARDS ON THE TABLE

You've decided that you must face up to the pain, heartache, stress and plain terror of being in debt. This is the first step – and as we discussed in the previous chapter, the most difficult one.

In the depths of the Second World War, London was being bombed on a nightly basis by Hitler's Luftwaffe.

Firestorms swept the capital.

Britain's Prime Minister was that immense historical figure, Winston S. Churchill. A journalist asked how he coped with the massive responsibility on his shoulders. How he managed the expectations of the British people.

"If you're going through hell," the great man replied, *"keep going."*

Churchill was a former soldier with combat experience. He knew that, when we're under fire, our instinct is to freeze. In fact, the best option is to keep moving forward.

And when faced with a problematic situation, our brain tends to multiply it a hundred times. It's an unfortunate habit of the human mind.

Did you ever go camping when you were a kid? You would wake up with a start on a dark and windy night. Convinced that you could hear footsteps outside. Or twigs breaking underfoot as some nameless beast roamed outside your tent. After a few minutes of terror, you would fall asleep and wake up to a bright and beautiful morning.

Those fears of the night seemed like what they were, the inventions of an overexcited mind.

Have you ever gone for a swim in a lake, river or sea and begun to imagine some terrible creature is under the water? Now, you know that the creature is a figment of your imagination. And yet, you make your way to shore at speed.

Once on dry land, you look out across the clear and calm water and think to yourself "Well, that was ridiculous!

The same is true of your debt fear. It keeps you tossing and turning in the dark night. Grinding through your mind with endless repetition. Sweating as you go through the day.

Face the fear for what it is. Take that step forward. And keep walking with head held high.

9. FACING THE FEAR

Many years ago, when I first started a 9 to 5, Monday to Friday job, I was like pretty much everyone else.

I looked forward to the weekend. But then the weekend came. And I looked ahead to the 'Monday morning blues.'

Come Sunday afternoon, I was already beginning to feel low. By Sunday evening I was a crotchety so-and-so who nobody wanted to approach. Like a bear with a sore head.

One Sunday evening, my wife told me that she'd had enough. I needed to address my weekly melancholy. I asked her how she was able to relax all the way through to the end of the weekend.

Here's what I do, she said. Every Sunday afternoon I spend 15 minutes writing in a notebook. I note down what I need to do the following week, starting with Monday morning.

A simple shopping list of tasks that I can clear when I hit the office. Once that's done I close the notebook, put down the pencil, and get on with enjoying the weekend.

So that's exactly what I did. I walked out of the house, went to the corner store and bought a pad and a pencil.

I took the pad and pencil home and sat at the kitchen table. I drew up a list of five tasks to complete when I got to the office on Monday morning.

In the next column, I scribbled down what action I was going to do to finish the task. Who I needed to call or meet with, what figures needed completing, and so on.

Then I closed the notepad and dropped it into my briefcase.

And at that moment, wonder of wonders, I felt a great load drop from my mind. Let Monday bring what it may, my brain seemed to be saying – I'm all set for it. Plans are in place. I'm ready for action!

I turned to my wife, smiling. "How are you feeling now honey?" she asked.

"Great, I replied – now let's go for dinner, my treat!"

After all, her advice had relieved the stress of many, many Sunday evenings.

So here's the thing. We can set out our debt problem in the same way.

I'm not saying that debt is of the same importance as my Sunday evening blues, but the principle remains the same. And I promise you that it works.

You've faced up to the problem of debt. You're determined to do something about it. Now, by laying it all out in front of you, you can begin to build a plan. And you can do this without fear.

Without fear, because there is nothing 'real' to fear. The fact that you are making this step demonstrates that you have decided to face down what fear you might have.

Make that crucial decision and you'll find that the fear melts away. Like the imagined monsters under the sea as you swim. Or the strange creatures outside your tent on your scout camp.

Once the sun comes up, the fear melts away.

Then, to quote Winston Churchill again, we *"may move forward into broad, sunlit uplands."*

10. TIME FOR A PLAN

General George S. Patton is one of the most successful generals who ever fought a war. His methods could be unorthodox, but they were effective.

There are many quotes attributed to General Patton. The one I find particularly memorable is this:

'A good plan executed with violence now is better than a perfect plan executed next week.'

For our purposes, I'm going to take *'with violence'* to mean *with urgency.* Though I'm sure the good General had something more aggressive in mind!

Patton meant that it's better to start right now and do something. Even if it's not perfect. Rather than think about it for too long and do nothing.

So let's start right now.

All we need is a pencil and a pad, or a sheet or paper.

Here we are, ready to 'face our fears'.

Remember when I went out and bought that notebook? That Sunday afternoon, I sat down at the kitchen table with a blank page before me. No one told me how to go about this.

So I took out my pencil and sketched out what seemed logical to me.

And this is what I wrote:
1. What do I need to do today?
2. What do I need to do in a week?
3. What do I need to do in a month?
4. What do I need to do in a year?

That's enough. If we can figure out our one-year goal, we'll be well on our way!

"Look after the dimes and the dollars will look after themselves." So my grandfather, a big City Hall treasurer, often reminded me.

While the essence of this saying remains true, of course, I'm taking the meaning of his words in a different way.

Now we have our four steps, for our purposes I'm going to ask you to reverse them.

The best way to approach debt is to start one step at a time. But we need to know what the final destination will be before we begin.

This is not going to be a journey into the unknown. We don't have time to be vague. We're not going to be walking into a fog. We need clarity and we need a goal.

Have you read *'Alice's Adventures in Wonderland'*?

On her travels in Wonderland, Alice comes to a fork in the road. A character called 'The Cheshire Cat' appears:

"Would you tell me, please, which way I ought to go from here?" asked Alice.

"That depends a good deal on where you want to get to," said the Cat.

"I don't much care where—" said Alice.

"Then it doesn't matter which way you go," said the Cat.

In our case, unlike Alice, we do know where we want to get to. We have a clear idea of the goal:

A debt-free life.

And we're ready to put a time on that.

Here are our four steps, *reversed:*

1. What do I need to do in a year?
2. To do that, what do I need to achieve in a month?
3. To make that happen, what do I need to do this week?
4. In that case, what do I need to do today?

What do we need to do in a year means, what is the big picture, what do we need to achieve? To look at it another way, what's the problem?

In our case, the problem is, we're sinking under a pile of debt, right?

Bills are following bills. Scary looking envelopes are piling up.

Unlisted missed calls are clogging up your cell.

Now they're leaving messages at your place of work.

Strangers are even calling at your home – and leaving calling cards when you don't answer the door.

So, here are two things we are *not* going to do:

We're not going to panic.

And we're not going to hide any more.
Here are two things we *are* going to do:
We're going to face the debt.
We're going to follow that simple four-step plan.
And then, we're going to feel a weight off our shoulders, heart and mind.
We're going to feel a huge sense of relief.
We're going to see the world in a different, positive light.
We're going to move forward one step at a time.
And we're going to be free.
We'll never again avoid picking reading the mail, answering the phone, opening the front door.
It is going to be a step forward to a different life.
You're now sitting at a table, pen in hand, looking a piece of paper with four questions on it. Four questions you have asked yourself.
Think of yourself sitting at the same table in a year's time.
This will give you a good chance of answering the first question.
What do you want to be your situation then? A year is a long time. It's 365 days after all!
At the same time, hasn't the past year flown by? What were you doing a year ago? Has anything changed?
Let's assume that your answer to the first question is, 'I want to be debt-free.'
To get to that point, what actions must you take in the next month, the next week, today?

By the way, let's be realistic. Your debts might be such that you know, deep inside, that a year is not enough.

That's OK.

Add another question. For example, where do I want to be in five years?

The sequence should remain the same though (5 years, 1 year, 1 month, next week, today). Try not to add all the years between. If you break it down too much, the goal will always feel out of reach.

Here's an example:

Question: Where do I want to be in one year?

Answer: Debt-free

Question: So where do I need to be in one month?

Answer: Have contacted each of my creditors (the people or organizations to whom I owe money). Have agreed an affordable repayment plan with them.

Question: So where do I need to be in one week?

Answer: Have drawn up a list of all my debts. Have made a chart of my income and all my outgoings (so that you know what pot of money you have to repay debts with).

Question: So what do I need to do today?

Answer: Buy a notebook, or set up a simple excel worksheet on my computer.

When we were toddlers, our moms cut up our food into small, bite-sized pieces. This made it much easier to swallow.

By approaching our food one bite at a time, we were able to finish a whole meal without drama.

The same thing goes for our debt. By breaking up the process into small steps, we'll reach our goal before we know it.

11. Know what you owe

I can tell you, from personal experience, that this is one of the most difficult things to face up to.
It sounds so simple, doesn't it? What do you owe? Such a short and easy question.
But hiding a deep, dark well.
So many of us think we know what we owe. Or, at least, we assume we know.

When we face up to the facts, we're surprised, or disappointed.

Don't fear this step though. Or, at least, don't fear to take the step.
This isn't about what you earn. And it isn't about your household or other regular expenses. We can come to that later (and I'm afraid it can be equally challenging!).
No, this is about the numbers that make you afraid, that keep you awake at night.
The figures that act like little gremlins, gnawing away for your attention.
It's time to face up
As Lailah Gifty Akita writes in *'Think Great: Be Great!'*
"To live for your dreams, you have to be fearless in life."

How much do you owe?

The first step is to assess how much you owe. Make a list of all your debts. Along with interest rates, outstanding balance, monthly repayments and due dates.
In this case, we first need to list what we owe.

Then we're going to list what we spend.
One step at a time though.
Who do you owe money to? I don't mean the regular bills that you pay on time. I mean the ones who are calling you and emailing you, asking for their money. The

brown envelopes you hide. The emails you delete. The calls you divert. List them in detail. Something like this:

Creditor Amount Owed Interest rate
AB Finance $200 15%
CDE Bank $700 12%
FGH Corp $400 20%

Don't worry about the total amount owed. That doesn't matter right now and will only cause stress! Focus on the individual amounts.

Look for any paperwork or letters you have from each organization. A recent demand letter, if you've kept them, is likely to state the amount currently owed. If you haven't kept any paperwork, you'll need to get a detailed picture of what you owe. Now would be a good time to call each creditor.

You don't have to get into a conversation with them at this stage if you don't feel comfortable doing that.

State a reference number and ask them for the total amount outstanding and the interest rate. They can't give you the information over the telephone? Ask them to email or mail you a current statement of the account.

They may want to ask some questions while you're on the call. In this case, state that you're putting a repayment plan together and will call them very soon to discuss.

How much do you spend?

Once you've completed your list of what you owe, it's time to complete the other half of the puzzle: How much do you spend?

This can be a little more difficult than it first appears. Some people note down everything they spend in a little notebook. Others keep every shopping receipt and update a spreadsheet on their computer daily.

Most people, though, do neither.

I used to have a good idea of my regular spending on rent and bills. But little idea of what went on other items. Groceries, irregular bills like car maintenance or gifts and nights out.

I would guess that most people are like me. We know what we *have* to spend, but have little idea where the rest of the money goes.

Which is one of the reasons we get into debt. We don't check our bank statement very often. When we do we're always surprised at what we see. And not in a good way!

Often our first clue that something is wrong comes at the ATM. We see 'Insufficient funds' and break out in a cold sweat. Our first instinct is to panic. Someone has been spending my cash! It must be fraud! We demand a bank statement right away.

Deep down though, we know we weren't burgled. We haven't been victims of 'cybercrime'. We spent the cash. We don't know how. We 'thought' there was enough to cover it.

If you've been keeping a notebook or a spreadsheet, you'll already have a good idea of what you're spending. If not, I would recommend starting that good habit. In the meantime, write down a list of everything you think you spend in a month. Start with the regular bills and then don't hold back.

Put in everything.

Weekly or monthly groceries.

Gas for the car. Coffees (and that regular chocolate muffin!) from the store.

Cigarettes and candy.

Include a monthly allowance for gifts, for birthday celebrations, for Christmas.

For clothes and shoes.

Add unexpected car repairs.

Anything that can leave your checking account in a month.

For regular annual bills, car insurance for example, split up the amount by 12. Make that amount part of your monthly outgoings.

N.B. Don't include any debt repayment, credit card payments and so on that you're already making in your list.

I'm going to repeat myself for added emphasis: This is the time to be honest with yourself. There's not too much point in going through the process if the numbers aren't as accurate as possible.

Have you covered everything you spend in a typical month? And allowed for a monthly allocation towards annual bills?

You're all set.

The Final Calculation

You have a good idea of what you owe. And you have a good idea of what you spend.

I hope you're feeling a little lighter already. The freezing dark fog that was filling your mind. That was causing you so much anxiety. That was paralyzing you. That was stopping you from moving forward with your life.

I hope that fog is lifting a little. Like when you see headlights ahead on a dark road. Or the sun breaking over the horizon after a long night. You can begin to see the way ahead.

The last calculation to make is quite simple, but it will give you a clear path to follow.

Take your income, monthly or weekly (a).

Subtract your outgoings, monthly or weekly (b).

The total (c) is what you can set aside to repay your debts.

$a - b = c$

This is the time to keep a cool head. Ask yourself once more if you have included everything you can in your outgoings (b).

Assuming all the numbers are on the table. It's time to get going!

What if the numbers don't add up?

It may well be that your personal calculation ($a - b = c$) ends up with a negative figure. This will be the case if you're spending more than you earn.

If this is so, then doing the exercise of putting all the numbers on the table has been a useful eye-opener. In rehab terms, it's been an 'Intervention'.

To paraphrase writer Charles Dickens' character, Mr. Micawber:
"Income $20, expenditure $19.99, result happiness. Income $20, expenditure $20.01, result misery"

You've been honest with yourself and can now see what's required. It was never going to be easy. But you've now done the groundwork and are in a much better place to start planning for the future.

If you're spending more than you make, or earning the same as you spend, you have no extra for your repayments. Then you have two options:

1. Minimize your expenses: Where can you cut back? This is a no-brainer for anyone dealing with excessive debt. You need to trim your expenses and stick to an austere budget.

    This will allow you to free up as much cash as you can to use towards settling your debts. It won't be for ever – now that you're committed to clearing your debts, the end will eventually come.

    That light you can see at the end of the tunnel? You'll be bathing in it! And when you get there, you will have set yourself up with some great habits for life.

2. Maximize your earnings: How can you boost your income?

    Don't ignore the income side of things. Look for ways to increase your regular income - or supplement it.

    Asking for a pay rise. Looking for a job that pays better. Taking on some freelance work or a 'side hustle'.

    Don't hold back! Any extra earnings can go a long way in helping you get out of debt faster.

Repayment Strategies

Now that you have your final calculation before you, you're ready to move on to the next step.

You are on schedule for 'Where do I need to be in one week'.

Soon you will start making contact with the people or organizations you owe money to. But there is still a little thinking to do first. This will ensure you have everything lined up before you make those calls.

Your contact with your creditors is likely to end in a negotiation of some sort. You want to win the negotiation. For the best chance, you must have every bit of relevant information at your fingertips.

In any negotiation information is key.

It was Francis Bacon, the English philosopher and statesman who said over 400 years ago:

"Knowledge is power."

With your list of creditors and your chart of income and outgoings, you now have a good handle on your situation.

Now you need a repayment strategy. There are several strategies to choose from. All will lead to the ultimate goal of zero debt. Your choice will depend on your circumstances. Which solution is best for you?

This step is important. Finding the right approach will help pay off your debts faster - and save you money. Here's a breakdown of some actionable debt clearing strategies:

Rank your repayments

If you're dealing with many debts, it can feel overwhelming to figure out what to tackle first. Which is why you need a strategy to rank your debt repayments.

The two most popular ways of prioritizing your debts are the 'Debt Stack' and the 'Debt Snowball'. They sound complicated, but are very simple.

The Debt Stack

With the Debt Stack method, list ('Stack') your debts in descending order of interest rates. So, the highest interest rate is at the top of the list.

Then you aim to repay that debt first.

You'll still be paying a small amount to your other debts. But the focus should be on the one at the top of the list.

That's because, having the highest interest rate, it's costing you the most.

The Debt Snowball

With the Debt Snowball method, you again make a list of your debts. But this time with the smallest total debt at the top of the list.

Here the focus is on paying off the smallest debt first. Whatever the interest rate.

Again, you'll won't ignore the other debts. You'll still be paying a small amount towards them. But the aim is to pay off the smallest one first.

Then, like a snowball gathering size as it rolls down the hill, you can move on to the next biggest one. And then the next.

Until you find yourself only paying off the biggest one.

Both approaches have their advantages. It depends on your preference. And what suits your character!

The Debt Stack can help you cut your interest costs. It will save you money in the long run.

The Debt Snowball can be more motivating. Because you clear the smaller debts first, you're checking off debts from your list faster.

Rearranging your debts

I enjoy doing jigsaw puzzles. I always have. It's something to do with the satisfaction of making order out of chaos. I love the process of re-arranging all those mixed up pieces. Making one beautiful picture gives me a feeling of great satisfaction and well-being. In fact, I would recommend a good jigsaw puzzle session to anyone!

It's time taken which clears your mind and allows you to focus on a particular task. I have worked on many jigsaw puzzles. But there is always the same feeling of anticipation when I first open the box. In front of me lies a pile of one thousand small pieces. All must fit together. I take a big deep breath, consider closing the box - and then get to it!

When you face up to your debts they can feel as much of a puzzle as a jigsaw. There are several methods you can use to get them into line before you start your repayment plan. These can also save you money during the repayment. You'll get a similar feeling to mind when completing the puzzle!

Here are 4 ways you can move your debts around to make repayments easier:

1. If you have credit card debt, consider opting for a balance transfer credit card. This will allow you to move your debt to a new card. Usually with the incentive of a zero-interest rate for a limited period of time. To make the most of this, aim to pay off most of the debt on the card inside the interest-free period.
2. If juggling several debts, look around for a competitive debt consolidation loan. This will combine all your debts, credit cards, loans etc, so that you have one monthly repayment. A debt consolidation loan is more manageable. But make sure that the interest rate is reasonable. The interest rate will be lower than your credit cards, but make sure to shop around for the lowest. And don't begin to build up further debt alongside the loan!
3. If you do have access to any savings, offer to make a lump sum payment towards your debts. This will most likely get you the best deal. I do appreciate that this is not an option available to everyone. Banks and finance companies are always willing to negotiate the debt down if you have a lump sum of cash to offer. Sometimes *way* down, if the debt is particularly old.
4. Work with a debt counselling/management company. For one reason or another, you may be unable to negotiate with the banks. Work with a reputed debt management company. They can negotiate on your behalf and help tailor a debt repayment strategy for you. Look out for an organisation that doesn't charge you for their work. You don't need to pay for someone to negotiate your debts. These organisations usually work for free, with a

charitable background.

And finally, I'm just going to repeat the magic formula: Minimize your expenses, maximize your earnings.

Remember, track your progress: Keep going. You can't get rid of debt overnight. Remember your 12 month or 5 year Plan. It takes time and a single-minded focus! Once you're on track with a repayment strategy in place, don't give up midway. Keep reviewing your progress regularly and re-strategize if your personal circumstances change.

Celebrate your successes. Like paying off a big credit card balance. And do whatever it takes to stay motivated.

12. THERE IS ALWAYS TIME

Creditors and debt collection companies (especially debt collection companies) will use certain tactics. The tone will be threatening and urgent. The need will be immediate. They want you to react now. This minute. Quick!

They also want you to panic.

Well, don't.

They'll get their money. You owe it to them, right? You understand that. You are happy to repay them for what you borrowed. Whether its credit cards or loans or energy bill payments. But now it's on your terms. Not theirs.

Why are they so urgent, so aggressive? In most cases, they get a commission for every cent they get back off you. And the sooner they get your money, the quicker they can take their cut and move on to the next job. So, they'll also want to persuade you that their debt is the most important, the one you need to pay off first.

Well, that's not the case. The repayment is in your hands, not theirs.

Never forget that the expression 'time is money' works both ways. The quicker you react, the less painful and more reasonable the repayment process will be.

Acknowledge their request, never ignore them. Talking to them, or at least writing to them buys you 'good' time. This demonstrates to them that they're going to get something without too much of a fight.

They can keep the tough stuff for someone else. Why should you have to put up with that? Ignoring their demands causes things in their world to escalate

This is when an email becomes a letter becomes a phone call becomes a house visit.

You may feel that ignoring them is buying you time, but all it's doing is storing up a more trouble for later.

Think of a giant dam, like the Hoover on the borders of Nevada and Arizona.

The mighty construction holds back a river or a reservoir.

In winter the river or reservoir fills up. And the flood of water coming through the dam needs controlling.

Otherwise it would rip through the strongest concrete. Causing untold damage to the surrounding area.

We need to do the same with our creditors. A short word now will save a lot more trouble later. Once they realize that, one way or another, you intend to pay, the pressure eases a little.

Remember also the saying, 'the squeakiest wheel gets the oil first'. Your creditors are relying on shouting loudest to ensure that they get paid first. They're fooling you. Everyone will get their drop of oil. But in your time. Their priority is not your priority.

You are in control, not them. Ultimately, you have something they don't have. They can shout and curse and cause all kinds of trouble, but you're in control, because you have all the information.

As the great Benjamin Franklin wrote *"By failing to prepare, you are preparing to fail"*.

You have prepared thoroughly.

You have done your homework.

You know exactly what your weekly or monthly income is.

You have your outgoings and how much you need to spend on each. You have taken note of everything.

You have subtracted the outgoings total from the income total.

You know the exact amount you can 'reserve' for repayments.

Creditors will try and make you agree to the highest regular repayment they can get.

But this makes no sense if it's more than your 'reserve'.

And you may have more than one creditor. The 'reserve' has to cover them all.

They will also try to make you repay the entire sum owed.

But again you have the upper hand.

After all, the creditor wants their money. And only you have the means to give it to them. Without your cooperation, they'll never get a cent.

If you're tempted to fall in line with your creditors' first demand, remember the priorities:

Address the immediate and basic needs for you and your family. This means covering food, electricity, water and gas bills. Then the rent or mortgage. Then – finally – loans and credit cards.

Now agree a reasonable payment plan with your creditors. One by one. Get their agreement in writing.

We're moving forward now.

13. TALKING IT OVER

There was a long-running ad campaign for a telephone company in the UK during the 1980s. They ads were encouraging people to use the phone more.
The slogan reminded customers that *"It's good to talk."*
If there's one big lesson I took from a lifetime of debt, it's that talking to someone about the problem eased the burden.
You know the saying *'A problem shared is a problem halved'*? Well, it's true.
Talking about debt won't make it go away. But you'll feel a ton of weight fall from your shoulders as soon as you share your story.
You may be thinking "Why should I stress them out with my problems?" Well, believe me, those problems are far, far better 'out' than 'in'.
In most cases, people are glad to help, even if it's by listening.
And once you know that somebody else knows, you can begin to bounce ideas and strategies off them. You might even find that they've had similar problems themselves in the past. Or they may have problems right now, like you.
And are more than willing to pool possible ways forward. And even if they haven't, they will still have ideas and suggestions that will prove valuable.
This person could be a close friend, family member, partner, spouse, colleague or pastor.
They should be someone who knows you well. I mean, you could tell a stranger on the bus. But that wouldn't be of long-term benefit. Beyond them throwing you some quick advice which wouldn't always be in your best interests.
An individual who knows you will take the effort to give you considered advice. They don't want to see you fail.
A further point. If you have a partner, the debt may have been putting a strain on your close personal relationship. The other person affected is the first person you need to talk to about it.
Now. I know. This will also be the most painful. But do it. You cannot shoulder

this burden alone.

If your income is sustaining a household, then the debt will affect them too. Sharing the problem may also allow them to adjust their spending habits to help ease the debt. Believe me, if you have a strong partnership, this will survive – even stronger.

Again, you may find it helpful to discuss the debt with a professional debt counselling service. Bear in mind that this service is usually provided free. There is no use in spending money on debt counselling! That makes no sense!

At the very least, debt counsellors will help you to put an income and repayment plan together. They will tell you how to contact creditors. And provide you with a strategy to address the immediate problem.

Some debt counsellors will even take on the burden with negotiating with creditors on your behalf. Some creditors, especially larger organizations, will appreciate this because it shows that they have a strong likelihood of getting most of their money back.

In the end though, whoever you talk to, do it soon. Today if possible. Problems caused by debt will only grow if you keep them in the dark. My debt became a problem because I tried to deal with it all by myself. For much of the time, this meant doing nothing at all. When I shared my situation, actions and consequences followed, leading towards repayment.

14. REELING IT IN

When you're going through the process of unburdening yourself of debt, it's very easy to neglect one key person. You get so busy making arrangements with debtors. Putting your financial affairs into order takes up time. It's easy to overlook a key component of the journey.

Make your plan to clear the financial obligations that are holding you back. But put one person at the center of everything.

Who's that one person?

You.

Without you, the plan will fail. Only you will be able to ensure that the plan happens. That every step forward occurs.

All the way to a successful conclusion.

For you to be in a position to make that happen, you and your family need to be healthy. Eating well. Clothed. Living under a decent roof.

Yes, your debtors are chasing for payment. Each feels they are your priority. Each cries that the sky will fall on your head if you don't pay up.

Well it won't.

But unless you're looking after yourself first, none of them will get a bean.

15. COMING OUT STRONGER

In the world of addiction, it's accepted that 'survivors' are never 'cured'. They have learnt to control their constant craving. For alcohol, tobacco, drugs or even sex. But it is only dormant. The addiction is waiting for the least opportunity to rear its ugly head again. To jump straight back out. At any time. For the rest of their lives. Former addicts must learn to live with the fact that they will always be 'in recovery'. They can never feel comfortable that they have 'recovered'.

Take the time to read this quote from Heather King, author of 'Parched':

"I once heard a sober alcoholic say that drinking never made him happy. But it made him feel like he was going to be happy in about fifteen minutes. That was exactly it, and I couldn't understand why the happiness never came. Couldn't see the flaw in my thinking. Couldn't see that alcohol kept me trapped in a world of illusion. Procrastination. Paralysis. I lived always in the future, never in the present. Next time, next time! Next time I drank it would be different, next time it would make me feel good again. And all my efforts were doomed because already drinking hadn't made me feel good in years."

The circumstances that force every individual into debt are many and varied. Everything from a sudden family medical emergency to loss of a steady job. Many times, this is out of our control. We need the money to put something right – and that might mean a life or death situation, not a new coat.

As we discussed earlier, being in debt can be addictive.

Or rather, spending more than one earns is very, very easy to do.

We may spend months or years clawing ourselves out of debt. And back into the light of debt-free life.

But it can be very easy to fall right back.

Here's Al Pacino again. This time as Michael Corleone in *'The Godfather Part 3'*:

"Just when I thought I was out, they pull me back in!"

A climber eases themselves up the sheer mountainside. After hours and hours of inching up the sheer rock, they are about to reach out to the final handhold.

Then they see a beautiful little flower – a rare Alpine Edelweiss.
It's out of reach, but the temptation to reach out for it is too great. In reaching out, the climber slips and falls, way back down to their last marker.
And so, they have to start up all over again.
Your goal is the top of the mountain. The little flower that is out of your reach is tempting you to fail. To fall.
Don't be that climber. When you have put all the hard hours in. The blood, sweat and tears. The stress and the tension and fear behind you.
Decide that you will do your best never to let debt happen again.
You owe it first to yourself and then to all those who may care for you.
When you feel like you're sinking in the middle of a debt swamp, it doesn't feel as if anything positive can ever come out of it. It doesn't feel that there is an end in sight.
A light at the end of the tunnel. A new dawn on the horizon.
But here's the strange thing. Something unexpected. When you have cleared your debts. When you are free of that financial, emotional, mental, physical burden. When you've got used to your shoulders not sagging. Your head not dropping. Your pulse not racing when you think about money. After it's all over. You're going to come out stronger than ever before.
And you are going to be free.
Elon Musk grew up in South Africa. As a boy, he had a dream. And, boy, this wasn't a small dream.
Many of us started off wanting to go into space. Musk decided very early on, he was going to make it to Mars.
When, later on, he planned his career, every step of his plan aimed at leading to his dream. Along the way, he spent a lot of time in serious debt, with no way out. With sheer tenacity, dogged persistence and a 'never give up' attitude, he moved forward.

Musk's involvement in PayPal and other tech ventures made him his first billion. That funding led him to develop Tesla, the electric car manufacturer. But he never lost sight of his childhood dream.

So he moved heaven and earth to create SpaceX. The first private company to send commercial payloads into space.

The ultimate goal? Mars, of course.

Says Musk:

"We're going to make it happen. As God is my bloody witness, I'm hell-bent on making it work."

Our dreams may not be of reaching Mars, but they're as important to us. For most of us, paying off our debt and having the pure, blessed relief of living our lives debt-free, is our Mars. And that's OK, that's more than OK.

As Musk says:

"If you wake up in the morning and think the future is going to be better, it is a bright day."

Think of the bright day ahead. Every day. And every night before you turn out the light.

Remember the earlier advice? Write it down. Why is tomorrow going to be bright? Brighter than today?

And when is the brightest day going to be? When you reach the light at the end of the tunnel.

When the debt darkness is behind you. When you step out.

When you step up into the bright sunlight of debt freedom.

And once you are free of debt, your mind will be clear. Sharper than it's been for a long time.

The experience you have been through will give you an edge.

You have been through a life-changing period. You will come out of it a different person from who you were before. In a good way.

A great way.

You'll be better equipped to go on with the next step in your life.

Base your decision-making on the lessons you have learnt. The things you have seen, the steps you have taken. The progress you have made.

The automotive pioneer Henry Ford said:

"Life is a series of experiences, each one of which makes us bigger, even though sometimes it is hard to realize this. For the world was built to develop character. And we must learn that the setbacks and griefs which we endure help us in our marching onward."

In every way, you will be stronger.

And then, you will feel able to look back, to take stock, to catalogue what you have been through. And use that strength to move forward.

One step at a time.

A series of unfortunate events or a long-term habit or a single catastrophe leads us into debt. None of us chooses to be in long-term personal debt.

You have chosen to get *out* of debt.

I wish you all the very best with your personal journey.

And I hope that in this short book I've been able to share some thoughts and ideas which will help you achieve the goal of a debt-free life.

www.ingramcontent.com/pod-product-compliance
Lightning Source LLC
Chambersburg PA
CBHW030543220526
45463CB00007B/2962